THE KNOT
HANDBOOK

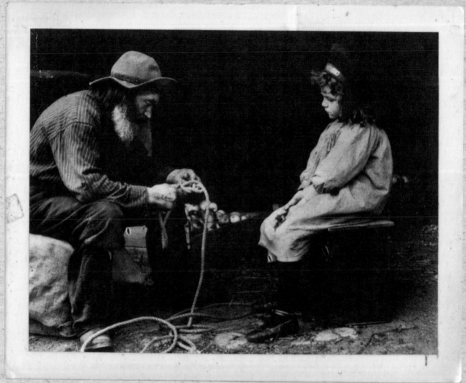

First published 2015 by Guild of Master
Craftsman Publications Ltd
166 High Street, Lewes, East Sussex,
BN7 1XU, United Kingdom
Copyright in the Work © GMC
Publications Ltd, 2015

ISBN: 978-1-86108-997-7

A catalogue record for this book is
available from the British Library.

Editor: Richard Wiles
Art editor: Rebecca Mothersole
Illustrator: Alex Bailey
Picture researcher: Hedda Roennevig
Colour origination by GMC
Reprographics
Printed in Turkey

THE KNOT
HANDBOOK

GEORGE LEWIS

CONTENTS

KEY

🛶 Boating

👟 Climbing

➕ Rescue

🌲 Arborist

⛺ Camping/Scouting

🐴 Equestrian

🎣 Fishing

🏠 Household

Introduction

To claim that almost anyone can tie a knot is a bit like stating that almost anyone can write or draw: it may well be true, but usually only up to a basic level. The difference between a roughly twisted line of hemp that just happens to interlace one or more pieces of rope and a beautiful and useful knot is the same as that between the most hastily daubed graffito and a Shakespearean sonnet or a painting by Monet.

This book shows you how to tie 50 knots. Some have been chosen for their fame, some for their beauty, and some because they are knots that everyone should know how to tie.

On every great theme, there are always possible variations and, as the text makes clear, from time to time people come up with new effective methods of tying. It may be that some of us are likewise destined one day to create knots that will bear our names for eternity, but before we can do that we need to study the time-honoured techniques: this intricate art has been practised for thousands of years and it can't be mastered in five minutes.

Many of the knots featured here are most strongly associated with – and probably originated from – sailing, but even the saltiest of them have extensive applications on land. Adhesive tape and Velcro have their uses, but they have not rendered knots redundant; no technological advance ever will.

GLOSSARY

Although the technical vocabulary is glossed where it occurs, it is worth defining some of the essential terms at the outset. These are as follows:

Standing part: the end of the rope that is held.

Bend: a knot in which one rope is connected to another or to itself after having been passed through something else, such as a ring.

Bight: a bend or coil in a rope.

Hitch: a knot in which one rope is connected to another or to an object.

Alpine Butterfly Loop

Also known as the Lineman's Loop, this knot is used mainly to make a fixed loop anywhere along a length of rope. It is most commonly used by climbers as a base for carabiners (metal loops with spring-loaded gates). Alpine Butterfly Loops are also sometimes employed to isolate frayed sections of a rope and thus extend its useful life. The main advantages of the Alpine Butterfly Loop are that it is more stable than a Bowline (see page 21) and easier to undo. On the down side, it cannot be tied with one hand.

The Alpine Butterfly Loop is one of the easiest knots to inspect, which is just as well because it is even easier to get slightly wrong. There is always a danger that a knot resembling the genuine article may in fact be a False Butterfly, which, as its name suggests, is unreliable.

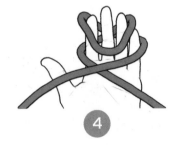

5

6

7

8

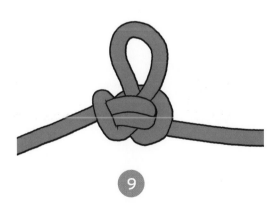

9

Anchor Bend

The Anchor Bend is similar to, but more durable than, a Round Turn and Two Half Hitches. It is used for tying a rope to a ring or anything similar. It is usually easy to untie, but may become jammed if subjected to extreme loads. This effect may be prevented by turning the rope an extra (third) time around the object to which it is tied and/or by finishing off with a Strangle Knot (see page 96) or a Constrictor Knot (see page 42).

The classic use of the Anchor Bend is in warping or kedging, a method of moving a sailing vessel by pulling on a rope attached to an anchor, a fixed object onshore or an adjacent boat. Landlubbers use it, too: it is among the most common knots, and one that everyone should know how to tie.

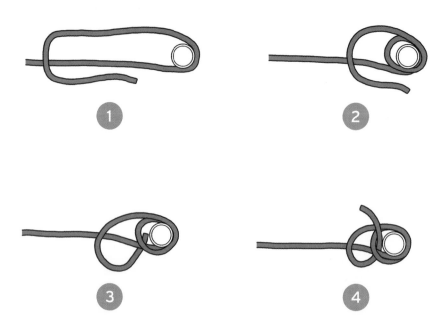

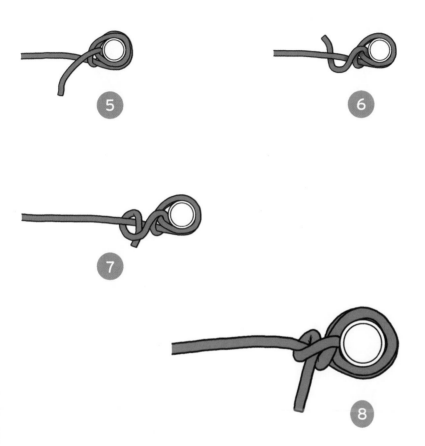

The knot's name originates from a time when 'bend' was understood to mean 'tie to', and was not restricted to knots that join rope ends.

Angler's Knot

This is one of the knots that all fishermen know – hence the name. Everyone should learn it because it's not too difficult and provides a host of benefits; it is, for example, very stable. It also lines up neatly with the standing part of the rope, causing no great lump or deviation in the general direction of the line.

  The loop formed by the Angler's Knot can be slipped over an upright pole to form a temporary attachment or a mooring. By enclosing the loop of one such knot around that of another on a different length of rope, it is easy to form rope chains that can be shortened or lengthened as required.

The Angler's Knot looks good and it's useful; that's why it's alternatively known as the Perfection Loop.

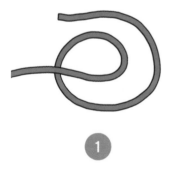

1

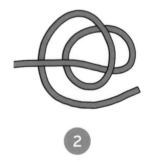

2

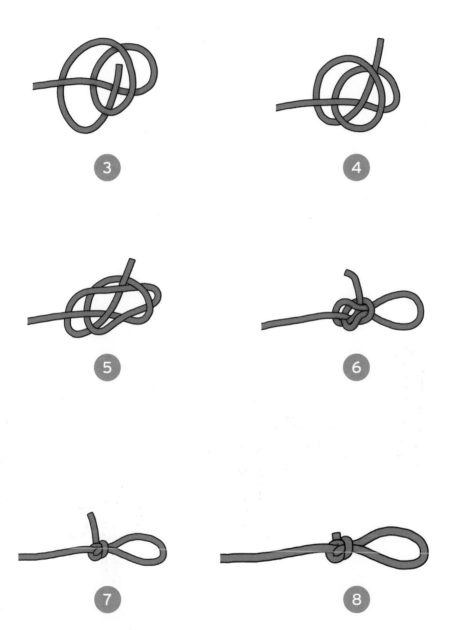

Ashley Stopper Knot

This is the classic knot for tying at the end of a rope to stop it from fraying. It's also known as the Oysterman's Knot, but its most usual modern name commemorates Clifford Ashley (1881–1947).

Ashley was an American artist who became fascinated with the practices of whalers off the coast of his native Massachusetts and who wrote several books about seafaring. His best-known publication, *The Ashley Book of Knots* (1944) is the most exhaustive study of the subject ever made.

Ashley may have fine-tuned the Stopper Knot, but there is no suggestion that he invented it: as a slightly variant form of the common Overhand Noose, it probably pre-dates recorded history; it has merely been renamed in his honour.

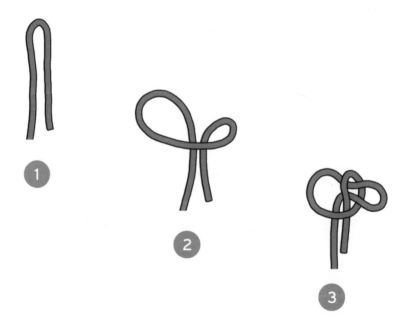

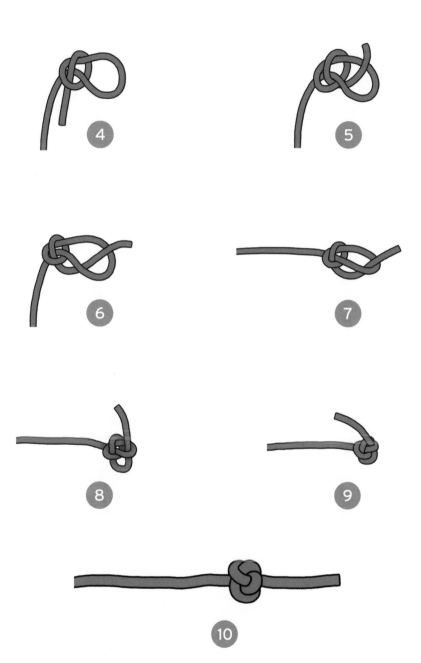

Blackwall Hitch

This knot is used to temporarily attach a rope to a hook and is most effective when the two have the same diameter. It tends to slip if placed under excessive strain, but this shortcoming is compensated to some degree by the ease with which it can be tied and untied. The knot relies on the friction created by the standing part lying over the end of the rope (step 2).

It is named for London's Blackwall Yard, which originally built tea clippers for the East India Company and later made battleships for the British Royal Navy and tugboats for the Port of London Authority. It was active for 360 years until it closed in 1987.

Adjacent to the Blackwall Yard were the premises of the rival Thames Ironworks and Shipbuilding Company; its works football team in 1895 became West Ham United, now a prominent professional football club.

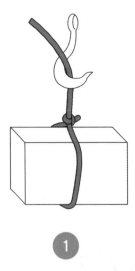

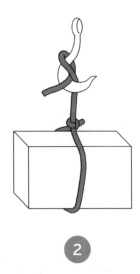

A view of Blackwall Yard in 1784, by the British maritime painter Francis Holman. When Holman painted it, this shipyard on the River Thames was said to be the biggest private yard in the world.

Blood Knot

This knot is used to join two lines of similar size and is a favourite of fly fishermen. Today it is most commonly used on nylon rope. Its strength increases in direct proportion to the number of loops made by each length of rope around the other: the recommended minimum is five; the maximum is widely held to be 14.

The basic Blood Knot is easy to tie, but getting it exactly right is rather more difficult, because it changes its structure when pulled tight. Ideally, when completed it should be symmetrical, with the loops around the meeting point of the two lines identical in appearance and of equal length. But as you may discover when you first try it yourself, this is easier said than done.

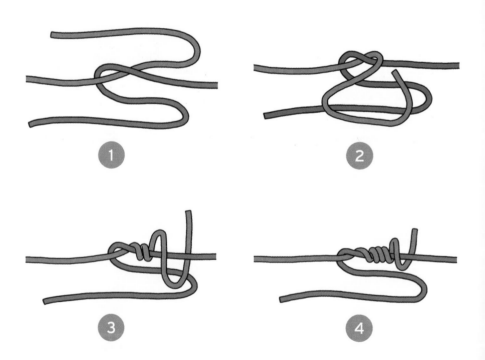

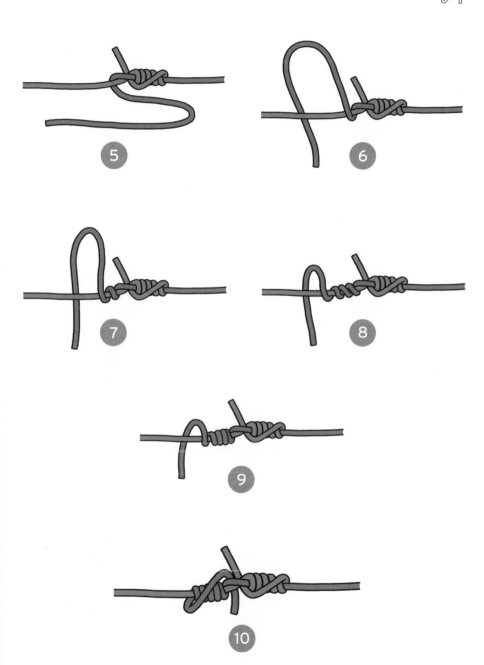

5

6

7

8

9

10

Boa Knot

This is the knot that you'll typically see in classrooms, lecture theatres and training suites tied around a marker pen and attached to the whiteboard or the flipchart to postpone for as long as possible the seemingly inevitable parting of the twain.

The Boa Knot is basically a variant and slightly extended form of the tried and trusted method known as the coil-twist-loop. It grips the object that you're scared of losing tightly, like the constrictor after which it is named. However, unlike the snake, which has a real feel for its victim, this knot is hard to make the right size… but not impossible, and the potential savings in stationery make it well worth the effort to learn.

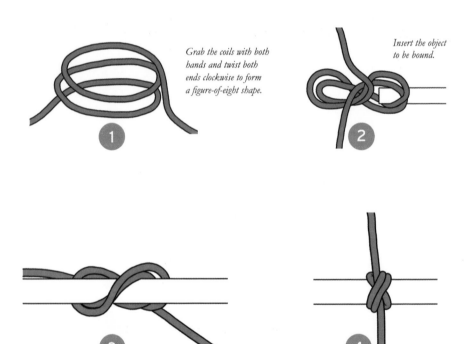

Grab the coils with both hands and twist both ends clockwise to form a figure-of-eight shape.

Insert the object to be bound.

Bowline

One of the most versatile knots in the world, the Bowline's predominant use is to fasten a boat's mooring line to a ring or a post, but it has a wide range of other uses, too. Everyone should know it, and it's easy to learn.

It's also easy to untie, although you should not try doing so while the rope is under pressure carrying a load. Neither is the Bowline any good as part of a safety harness unless it's supplemented by a Double-Overhang Strangle or Stopper Knot to prevent slippage.

Those reservations apart, the Bowline is a great knot that can be tied with one hand in case of injury or other emergency.

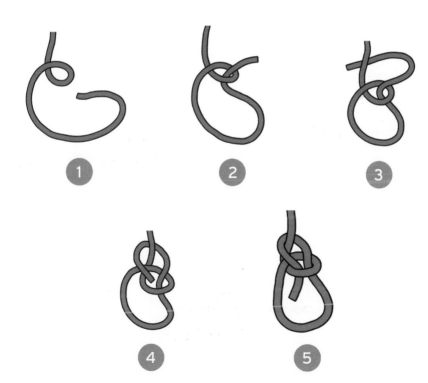

Bowstring Knot

There are numerous knots that can be used in a lasso (the Alpine Butterfly Loop, for example; see page 8), but this is the one used by real cowboys, who tuck the standing rope back through on the loop to make a snare that can be tightened with a deft flick of the wrist.

Today, Bowstring Knots are commonly associated with Wild West rodeos, but they're as old as civilisation itself: an ancient Egyptian wall painting of around 1,000 BCE depicts a hunter using one to rope in a bull by the horns.

The essential quality of the lasso is that the standing line should be free-flowing and capable of being tightened very quickly: there can be no snagging.

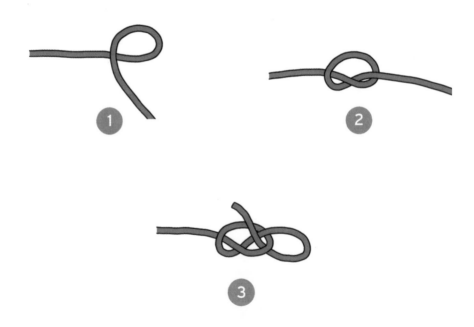

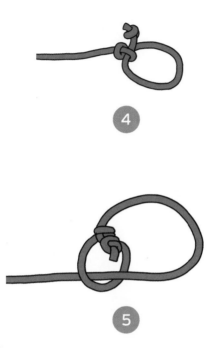

4

5

Most people who use the term 'lasso' are those who never work with one. Real-life cowboys refer simply to their 'ropes'.

Brummel Eye Splice

By no means straightforward – indeed, one of the hardest knots in this book – the Brummel Eye Splice is well worth the effort because ropes that end this way are quicker to tether and untether than almost any other attachments.

   The splice itself is intended to be permanent ('locked'); it's the loop at the end that makes the rope easy to connect and disconnect.

   Note that you will need a marlinspike or similar nail-like implement to make the requisite tunnels through the rope. The length of the tool will depend on the thickness of the twine. Most standard issue marlinspikes are between 6in and 12in (15.25 and 30.5cm) long, but the heaviest cables may require metal implements of up to 2ft (61cm) in length. It is easier to push the rope through the tunnels if the end is wrapped.

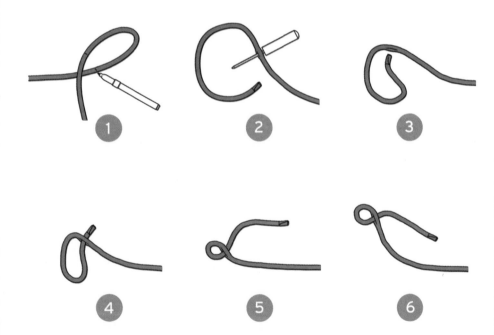

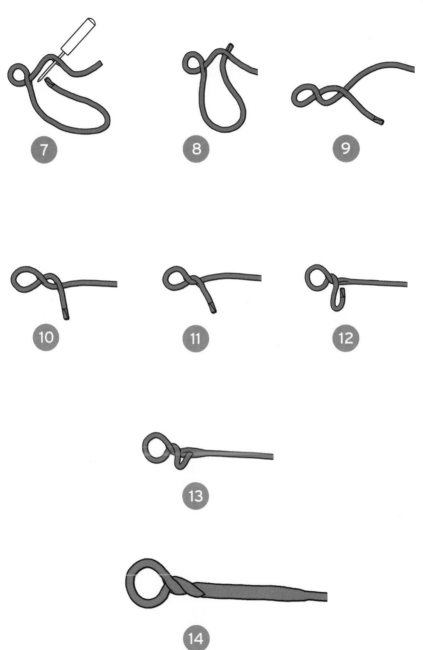

Buntline Hitch

A bunt is the baggy part of a full fishing net or a billowing sail. A buntline is a rope that passes from the foot-rope of a square sail to prevent it from bellying (puffing out) while it is being furled (folded).

A Buntline Hitch was originally the knot used to prevent bellying, but it also has wider uses in attaching a rope to any object. It is basically a Clove Hitch (see page 40) in which the turns are positioned so that they progress toward, rather than away from, the object.

The Buntline Hitch is most commonly seen as an attachment to metal rings. It is also the basic knot used for neckties.

The only caveat is that it is liable to jam when pulled too tightly, but this difficulty can be avoided by use of a slipped variant, a knot of the type often used to secure luggage racks to the roofs of cars.

Easy to tie, reliable and small, this knot's compactness enables the sails to be tied as closely as possible to the mast or rigging.

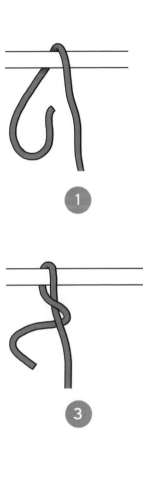

1

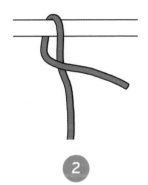

2

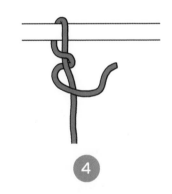

3

4

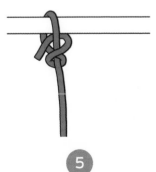

5

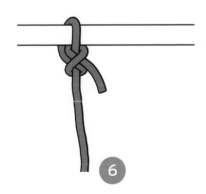

6

Carrick Bend

The etymology of the name is obscure, and may be either a corruption of 'carrack', a large galleon formerly used for carrying freight around the Mediterranean, or derived from the Carrick Roads seaways in Falmouth, Cornwall, the world's fourth largest natural harbour.

The Carrick Bend is used to join two ropes together. It is most commonly seen in hawsers (ropes that tie a ship to a quay), and may form the interstices of cargo netting and climbing nets.

A perfect Carrick Bend must have its tails diagonally opposite each other; in any other juxtaposition, the knot may come loose when pulled.

The Carrick Bend's symmetry has made it a popular device on coats of arms; in heraldry, it is known as a Wake Knot or an Ormonde Knot.

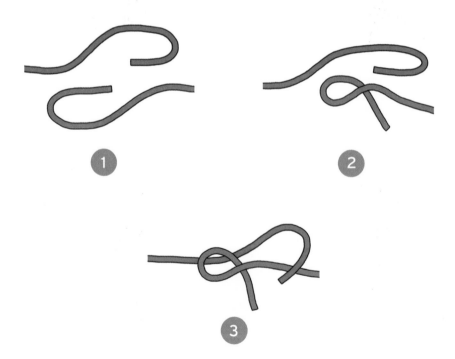

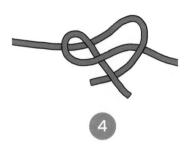

4

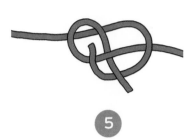

5

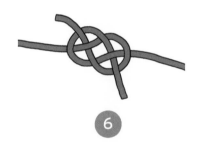

6

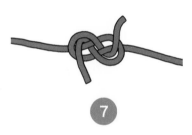

7

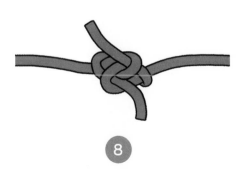

8

Cat's Paw

Through the use of a Cat's Paw, an object such as a crate can be secured on both sides by a single rope. When the loop of the rope is attached to a hook and lifted, the object will not swing around its own axis.

In order to achieve this, it is of course important that the loop should be exactly in the middle of the rope so that both sides are of equal length.

The name of this knot seems to derive from a misunderstanding: a cat's paw is, figuratively, a person used to do someone else's dirty work (from Aesop's fable of the monkey who used the paws of a cat to draw chestnuts out of the fire); the effect of this knot is much more like a cat's cradle, the pastime or game in which one person makes string figures around their hands.

This knot is often used by quayside crane operators and by game fishermen to attach lures to their lines.

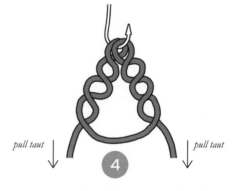

pull taut ↓   ↓ *pull taut*

Chain Sennit

Rows of knots of this type were originally used to shorten a rope, either while it was in use or for storage, or to prevent tangles during machine-washing. 'Sennit' or 'sinnet' is any flat braid or cordage made from several strands.

The application of pressure to one end shortens the chain by one link; pulling back the other end releases it altogether.

Long Sennit Chains are good looking, and so have been widely adopted in crochet and on dress military uniforms. Their other main advantage is that they are easier to tie than almost any other knot in this book.

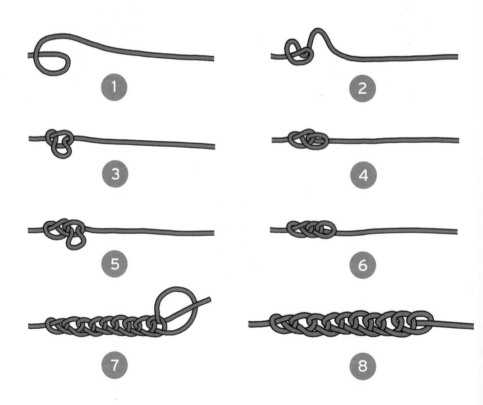

Mountaineers often use Chain Sennits, which are also known as Monkey Braid, Daisy Chains or Chain Stitch, to manage their ropes and prevent troublesome tangles.

Chain Splice

The classic maritime place of a Chain Splice is on the rope that holds the anchor chain and passes through the windlass (the wheel on the side of the ship's bow).

Its basic components are three strands of ropes of identical length and thickness that are plaited together, passed through the end link of the chain, and then braided again back along themselves for seven tucks before being sealed at the end with tape or a Constrictor Knot (see page 42).

Chain Splices are designed to take heavy loads, and as such may chafe over time. When this happens, the worn splice is cut off and the end remade a short distance further up the rope.

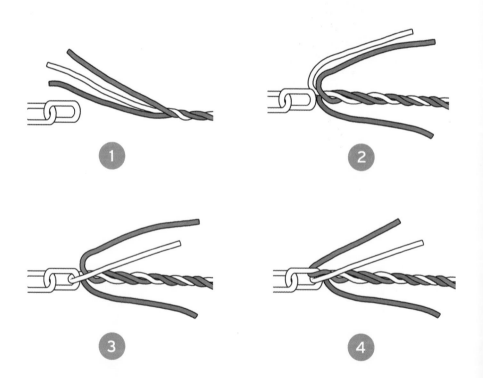

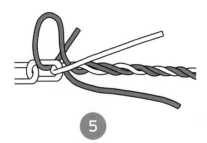

5

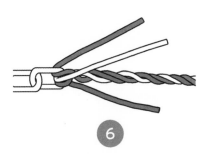

6

7

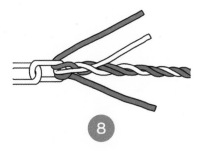

8

9

10

The Chain Splice is typically used in the anchor chain and rope combination that passes over a windlass and then descends into a chain locker in the forward part of the ship when the anchor is secured for sea.

11

12

Repeat for seven tucks then seal ends with tape or a Constrictor Knot (see page 42).

13

Cleat Hitch

In seafaring parlance, a cleat is any protrusion on a ship that may be used for tying the vessel to something else. A Cleat Hitch is a way of securing the connection; this knot is also used on halyards (ropes for hoisting or lowering a sail, yardarm or flag).

There is no consensus about how many loops are required for this knot, and although some people insist on a certain number, circumstances (and rope quality) alter cases: sometimes one turn alone will be sufficient.

After making the required number of figure-of-eight turns, the Cleat Hitch may either be completed (locked) by securing it to the standing rope or run on for attachment to another object.

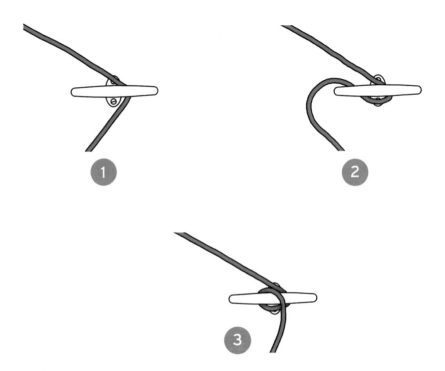

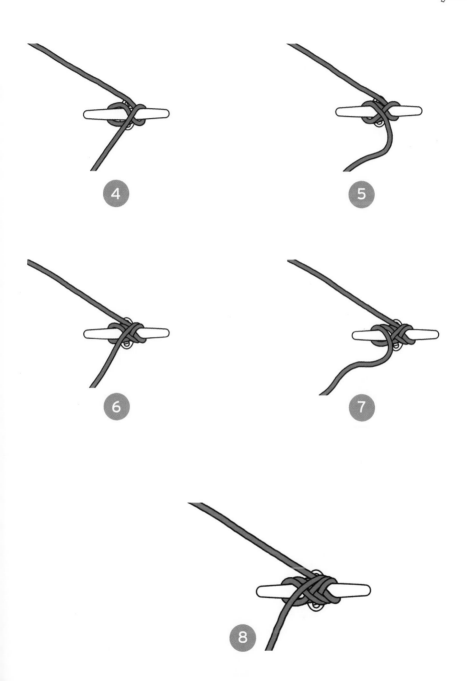

Clove Hitch

Known by numerous other names, including the Boatman's Hitch, the Builder's Knot, the Double Half Hitch, the Peg Knot and the Steamboat Hitch, the Clove Hitch is undoubtedly the most widely used, and possibly the best, knot for tying a stiff, thick rope because it never makes a sharp bend. It is also used to start and finish lashings (the bindings that prevent a rope from unravelling into its component strands).

The disadvantage of the Clove Hitch is that it has a tendency to come undone if subjected to excessive strain. It is therefore not normally used on its own. Neither should it be used in multiples: a line of Clove Hitches together is liable to bind too tightly and become impossible to untie.

The most effective and durable complements to the Clove Hitch are a Round Turn and Two Half Hitches, a Rolling Hitch, a Bowline (see page 21) or a Cleat Hitch (see page 38); for short periods with relatively little stress, a Constrictor Knot is sufficient accompaniment.

A paradoxical little knot, the Clove Hitch is liable to slip when under excessive strain and has an annoying tendency to bind, becoming almost impossible to untie.

Constrictor Knot

This loose knot, based on several figures-of-eight, is used by mariners to provide temporary bindings for the fraying ends of ropes and for keeping the end of a rope together while it is being whipped. On land, it is widely used to tie the necks of sacks or bags, and to hold two items together while they are being glued.

The Constrictor Knot provides many benefits, but has two major limitations. One is that it works only on curved surfaces that will grip it; the other is that it may tighten so much that it can be undone only by cutting the rope.

There are two variant forms of this knot: for knots that will never need to be undone, Double Constrictors are used; for those that are needed only temporarily, the Slipped Constrictor is preferred (although that, too, may be a devil to release).

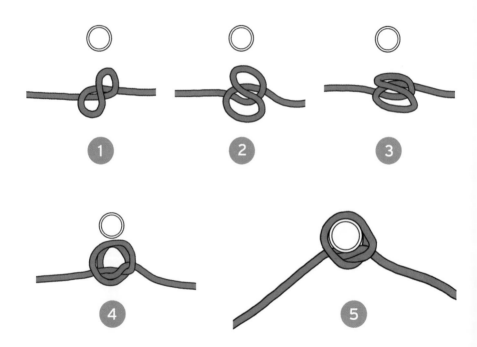

Cow Hitch

The Cow Hitch is similar to the Clove Hitch (see page 40), but sufficiently different from it to warrant separate inclusion here. It is also like the Girth Hitch (aka the Strap Hitch and the Bale Sling Hitch), which is the most commonly used method of tying two elastic bands together.

Its name is thought to derive from the discovery that cows could unwind the Clove Hitches that were traditionally used to tether them merely by walking around in circles, so this new knot was developed to keep them reined in.

The Cow Hitch is also used as an alternative to the Constrictor Knot by longbow archers to prevent damage to the bowstring when the arrow is released.

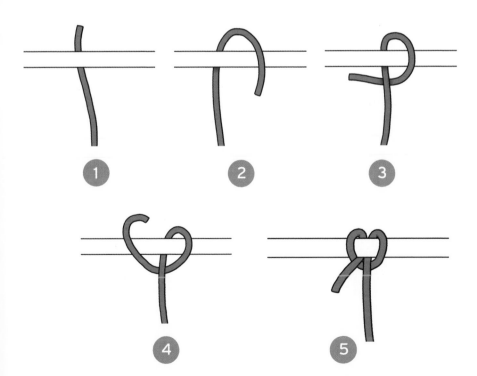

Double Dragon

The Double Dragon is a safe, strong and reliable knot that can be tied after the rope has been wrapped around the object to which it is to be secured: in that regard, it is unlike the Alpine Butterfly Loop (see page 8) that it most obviously resembles.

One potential problem with the Double Dragon is that it may become difficult to untie when placed under heavy strain; it is therefore not recommended for use in the middle of a line. Against that, pairs of Double Dragons are good for tying together two ropes of unequal thickness. They are also useful components of any multi-loop knot.

This knot divides opinion: some people wouldn't dream of using one, but aficionados say it's quicker than any other knot to tie and just as effective as most others.

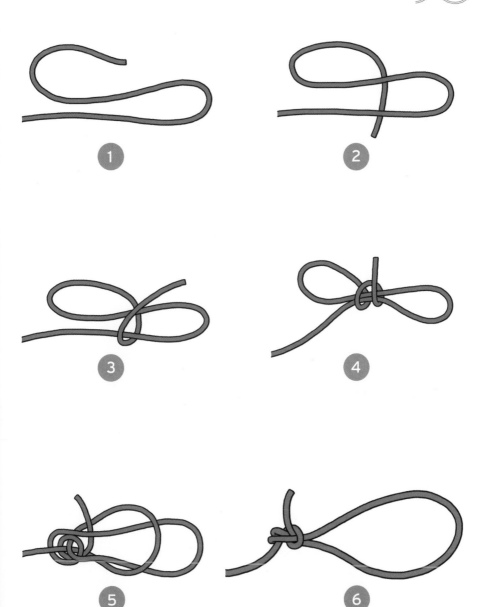

Double Fisherman's Bend

Also known as a Bucket Hitch or a Grapevine Bend, this knot is ideal for tying a lanyard (a short rope) fast to a handle or for any other similar purpose.

It is strong and reliable and often used in abseiling, but users must either tie it themselves or check it before setting off: where lives are at stake, take nothing on trust and leave nothing to chance.

The Double Fisherman is widely used to join climbing ropes, but it is not necessarily the best option because of its tendency to jam. One of the preferable alternatives may be the Zeppelin Bend (see page 110), which is easier to untie. Another is the Threaded Figure Eight (see page 102): although some mountaineers shun this knot because of its bulk, it is the easiest of the three to inspect.

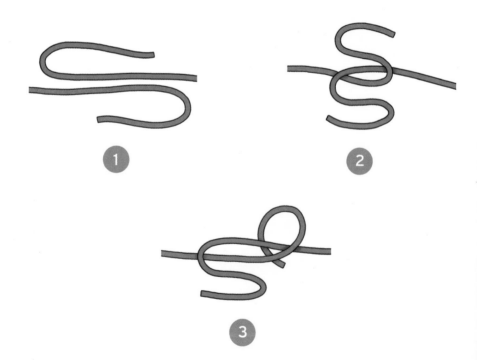

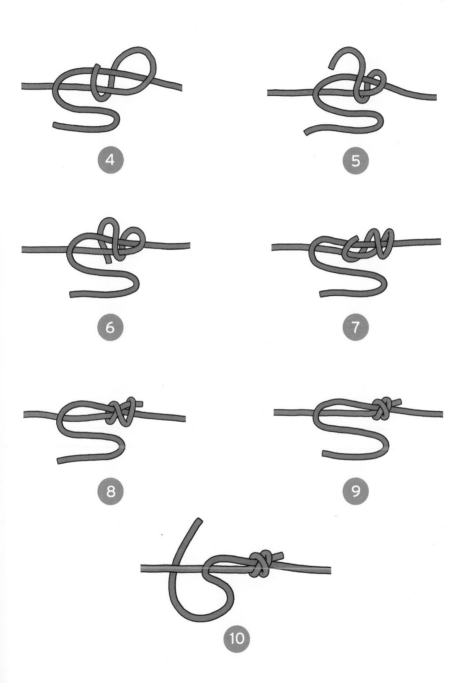

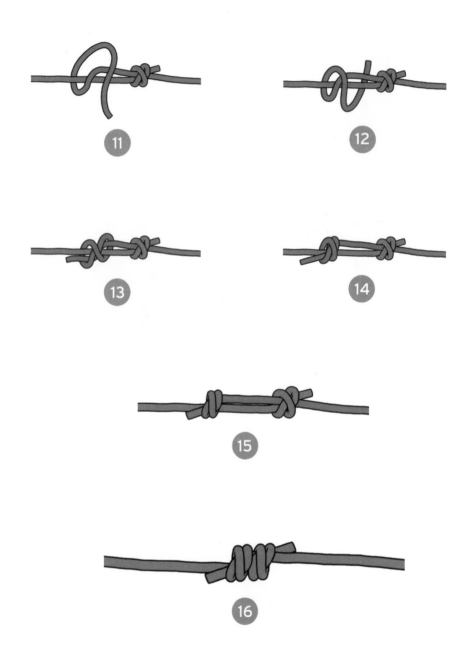

Climbers rely on strong knots like the Double Fisherman's Bend when belaying down a rock face, but will always check the knots first – when it comes to safety, nothing is left to chance.

Eye Splice

This knot – alternatively known as the Bargee's Eye Splice – is an amazingly neat and beautiful way of preventing the end of a rope from fraying.

The first step in its creation is to unravel the strands at the end of the rope. This isn't always possible by hand, and in such cases the classic instrument for separating them is a fid (a conical pin of hard wood). You can also use a marlinspike (see page 24) or a needle, or tape the ends of each strand to provide something to pull on.

Having separated the strands, start plaiting them as shown in the diagrams. With real rope, the Eye Splice may be achievable in very few tucks, perhaps only two, but modern synthetic rope is slippery and may require at least five and possibly as many as seven tucks. Nevertheless, the method is the same no matter how many times it needs to be repeated.

In a perfect world, all the rope will be used up in the splicing and you'll get a neat end. In the real one, however, it is likely that some strands will be longer than others. If that's the case, you can burn off the excess before tarring the end.

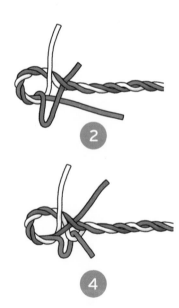

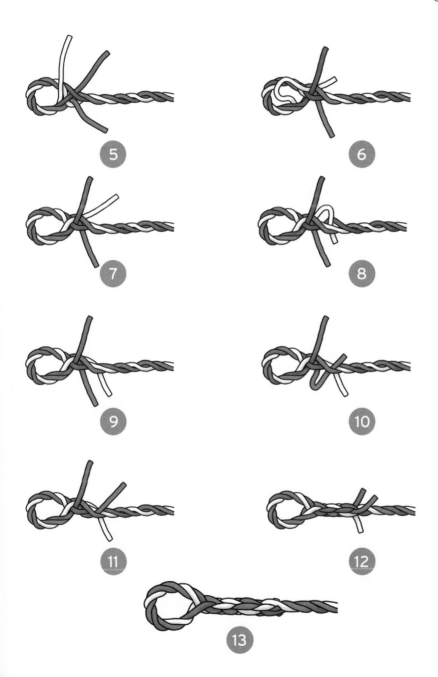

Half Hitch

This is a simple knot that can be used to tie a rope around almost any object.

Although two Half Hitches make a Hitch (often known as a Clove Hitch, see page 40), the latter is seldom used. The first Half Hitch is nearly always followed by a second to make the knot secure. That is the final step in the diagrams here.

The Half Hitch does not jam and is used in French whipping, a method of stopping rope ends unravelling and of providing grip over horizontal bars such as railings.

When several hitches are used together, the rope should always be passed the same way each time.

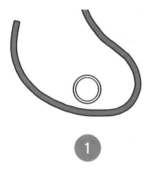

1

2

3

4

pull taut

5

6

7

8

Handcuff Knot

What's in a name? Not a lot in this case: the Handcuff Knot may resemble the linked metal bracelets used by police to restrain ne'er-do-wells, but it would take no David Blaine to get out of it.

Thus it is no good as a reliable harness, but that does not make it useless: its great merit is in saving people who are trapped outside the rescuer's line of vision. Imagine, for example, that you're hauling a potholer to safety: if you can't see the person where he or she is trapped deep underground, your instinct may be to respond to any resistance by pulling harder on your end of the rope. But what if the potholer has come up against an immovable object? Your tugging may crush him or her. In such a case, a Handcuff Knot would enable the person in trouble to loosen or tighten the knots around his or her wrists as necessary: it's a survival factor.

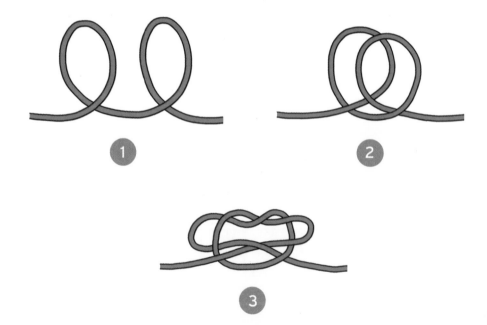

4

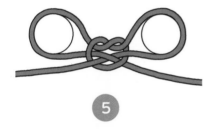

5

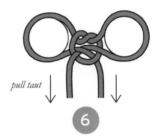

pull taut ↓   ↓

6

7

Klemheist Knot

The Klemheist Knot is used to tie a rope to a guy rope in such a way that it can move one way along the static line but not the other. It is a variant of the Prusik Knot (see page 80). The name comes from Dutch: klem, meaning 'clip'; and heist, meaning 'lift'.

There are two popular related types of Klemheist. One, also known as the Autoblock, the French Prusik or the Machard Tresse, has a carabiner (a metal loop with spring-loaded gates) at both ends of the movable rope. The other, the Bachmann Hitch, has a carabiner inside the basic hitch.

Knots that slide like this are known generically as friction knots. What they all have in common is that they are made of thinner rope than the lines to which they are attached.

Start with a Triple Fisherman's Knot. This variant is produced by making a third turn on a Double Fisherman's Bend (see page 46).

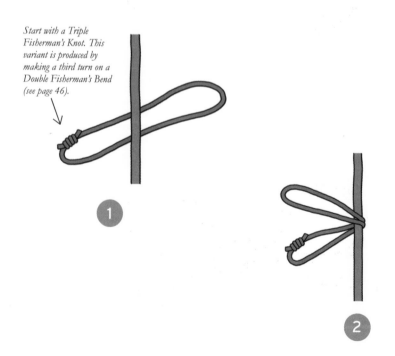

KLEMHEIST KNOT

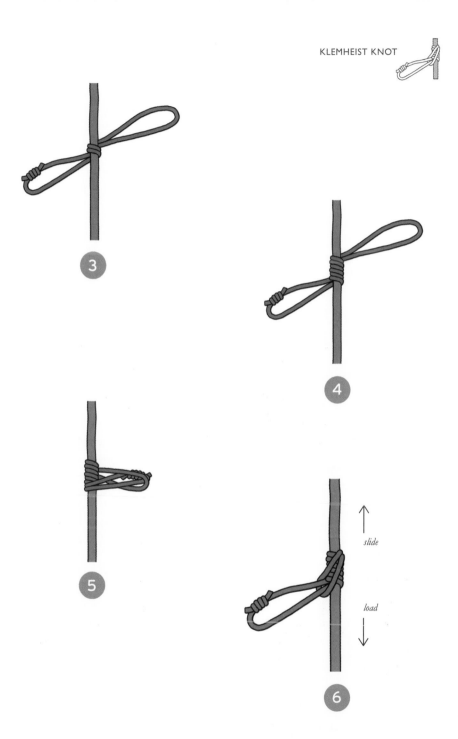

3

4

5

6

slide

load

Lanyard Knot

Anyone who labours under the misapprehension that knots are purely functional and have no aesthetic value should check this one out. It is a decorative knot that forms the eye of cords used as fastenings or handles or for hanging knives or whistles around the waist or neck.

The Lanyard Knot is a development of the Carrick Bend (see page 28) in which the two ends are brought round and up through the centre of the basic knot.

When tied in series, Lanyard Knots can produce beautiful patterns as double diamonds, diamond hitches or diamond plaits.

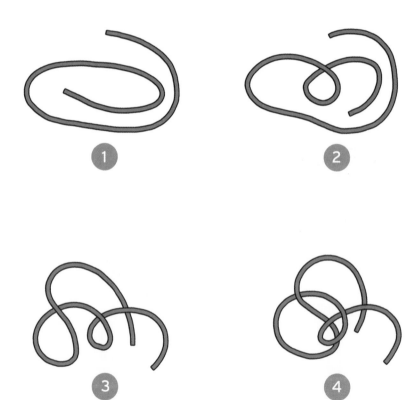

5

6

7

8

9

10

Lighterman's Hitch

As can be seen from the diagrams, the Lighterman's Hitch is perfectly straightforward to tie, consisting as it does of no more than a series of doubleback loops finished off with a Half Hitch.

But don't make the mistake of assuming that the effectiveness of knots is directly proportional to the difficulty of tying them: this one is widely used for towing heavy objects and for tying up to bollards, posts or winches.

Also known as the Backhand Mooring Hitch or the Tugboat Hitch, its only limitation is that it is of little use unless under strain.

This knot is easy to release, even under a weight, when the load can be controlled as the knot is loosened, and thus preclude slippage.

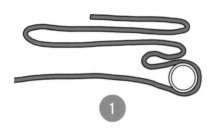

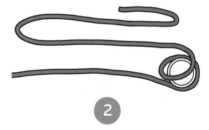

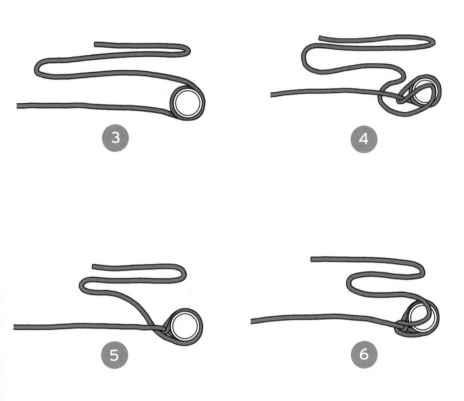

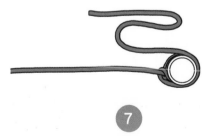

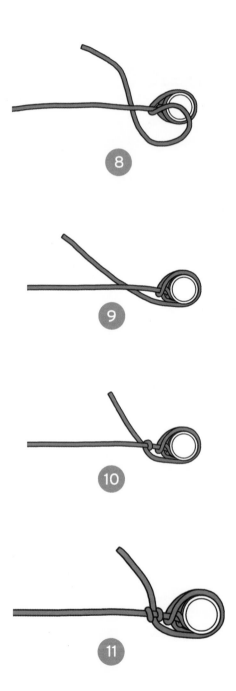

Lover's Knot

This knot joins two ropes so that they lie closely together in parallel and thus remain flexible but inseparable.

In practical terms, the Lover's Knot is similar to the Angler's Knot (see page 12). It is used to join two lanyards. In symbolic terms, it is even more important as a representation of everlasting affection.

Sailors who were leaving home on long voyages would give their girlfriends rings made from two strips of metal – one of them often gold – interlinked in this way. In folklore, courting couples would tie a Lover's Knot to a sapling: if the binding remained intact as the tree grew (and there was no reason why it wouldn't: it's a sturdy binding), that meant they would be together forever.

Closely related are rings that comprise two interlinked loops (tori) that revolve around each other but cannot be pulled apart.

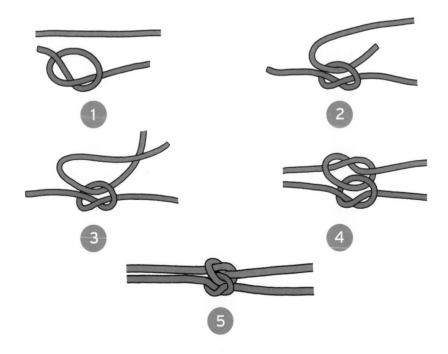

Man Harness Knot

This type of knot is used in series at equal intervals along a rope so that several people can get a firm grip and pull it.

In principle, the Man Harness Knot would be useful for participants in tug of war, but in practice this knot is banned from that sport because it takes some of the skill out of it: if there's no danger of slipping, it's less of a competition.

It is important to be aware that this knot will work only for as long as there is something – typically a human hand – inside it. If left empty, it will contract when pressure is applied to the ends of the rope. Thus it is less reliable than the similar Alpine Butterfly Loop (see page 8).

Man Harness Knots are known alternatively as Artillery Loops because they were used by soldiers to haul field guns.

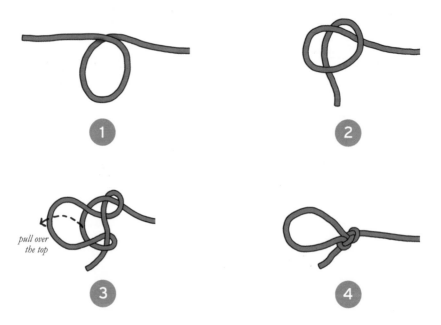

pull over the top

Tug of war, a sport from which the Man Harness Knot has been banned.
The knot prevents slipping, taking some of the challenge out of the event.

Marlinspike Hitch

A marline is any light rope, typically of only two strands, that is used to bind larger ropes. In general nautical terms, the spike is the tool used to separate them, but in the case of the Marlinspike Hitch it refers to the wooden or metal rung of a rope ladder, which is where this knot is classically found. It is also widely used around poles and moorings.

When using this method to make steps, it is vital to note that if a Marlinspike Hitch is tied correctly it will tighten when someone stands on the rungs; if it is tied the wrong way, it will form a slip knot that loosens on the application of pressure.

It is also important to ensure that each of the rungs is horizontal: if they are at an angle, they may slip sideways out of the hitch.

Any ladder made in this way must be tested before re-using after it's been in storage to make sure that it's still safe.

Use natural-fibre twine when whipping natural-fibre rope as it will be less likely to slip off.

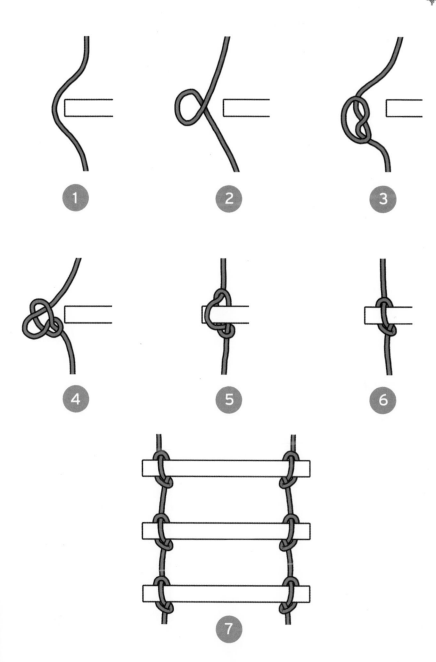

Midshipman's Hitch

This knot forms an adjustable loop for use on ropes under tension. It can be slid up and down, but tightens under pressure. Under its alternative name, the Taut-line Hitch, it is one of the six classic Boy Scout knots – the others are the Sheepshank (page 88), the Reef Knot (page 82), the Bowline (page 21), the Sheet Bend (page 90) and the Clove Hitch (page 40).

The Midshipman's Hitch is most commonly applied to the guy ropes of tents, but it is also used by tree climbers and as adjustable moorings in ports with a big tidal range.

On traditional rope made from hemp, the Midshipman's Hitch is the nonpareil – dependable and adjustable in equal measure. On modern synthetic rope, however, it may slip, a problem that can be avoided by the addition of an extra half hitch.

One of the intermediate stages in the creation of the Midshipman's Hitch is the Awning Hitch (step 6): this is a useful knot for campers because it will hold while the tent is being erected and can be tightened later by the addition of a final half hitch.

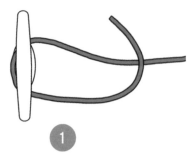

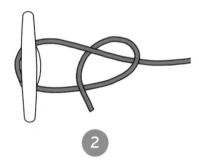

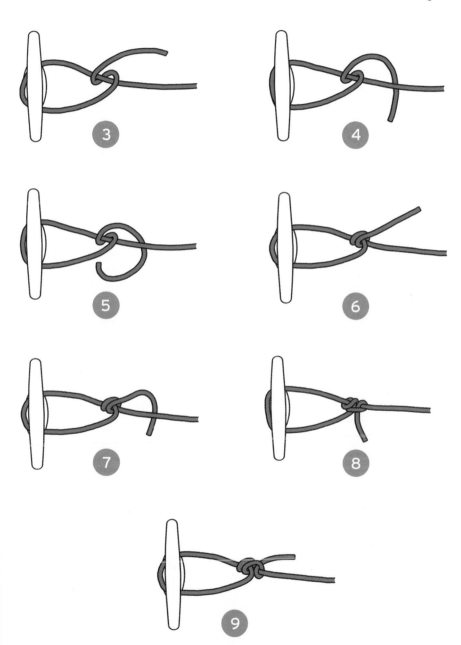

Monkey's Fist

The Monkey's Fist – named for its supposed resemblance to a clenched simian palm – is tied to the end of a rope to serve as a weight that makes it easier to throw in the manner of a slingshot or a hammer of the type used in field athletics.

At sea, Monkey's Fists are tied to heaving lines (used to haul boats in) at intervals of around 30ft (10m) to weigh the rope down. In this function, the knots are often, but not invariably, tied around stones or other heavy objects to provide further ballast.

The Monkey's Fist is a three-dimensional type of Borromean rings – three loops that are linked only for as long as they are all together: the removal of any one of them breaks the connection between the other two.

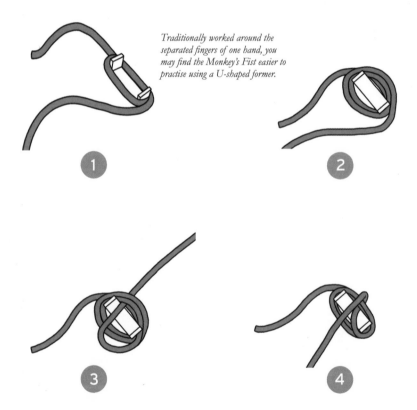

Traditionally worked around the separated fingers of one hand, you may find the Monkey's Fist easier to practise using a U-shaped former.

5

6

7

8

9

10

The Monkey's Fist is a decorative knot in appearance, but one that is also used to weight the end of a heaving line.

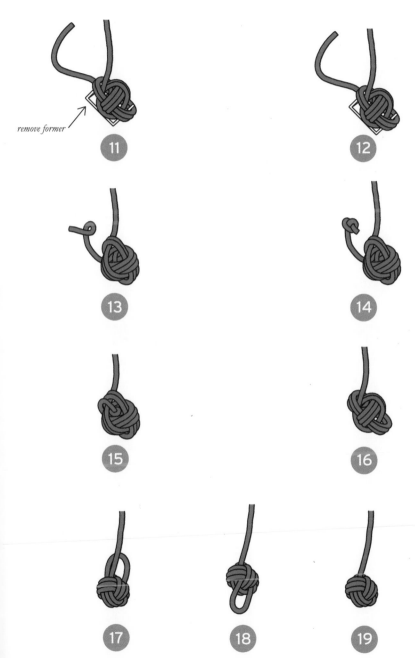

remove former

Myrtle Hitch

The basic format of the Myrtle Hitch is the same as that of the Constrictor Knot (see page 42), with the addition of a second rope that is threaded through the first. The two knots entwine around each other to form a right-angled hitch that can be used, like the Carrick Bend (see page 28), to make netting.

The etymology is unknown, but it may be speculated that it is used here as an alternative to 'clove', which in a botanical rather than a rope-tying context is the aromatic bud of flowers of the Eugenia genus of flowering plants of the *Myrtaceae* (myrtle) family.

This knot was dubbed 'Myrtle Hitch' after being introduced to the International Guild of Knot Tyers by knotmaster Mr Dave Root, and it is another form of one of the Carrick Bends.

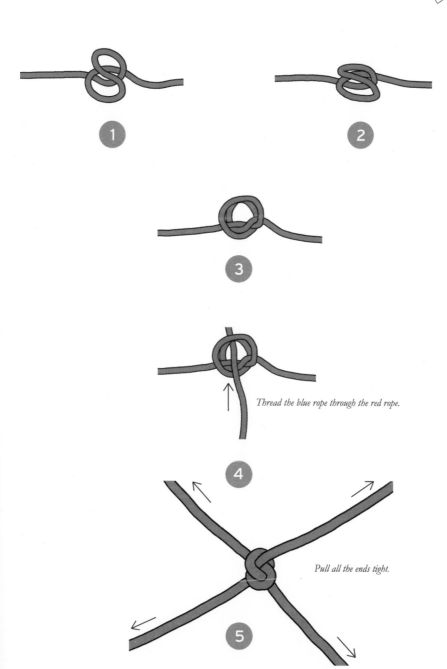

Thread the blue rope through the red rope.

Pull all the ends tight.

Noose

A Noose is a slip knot with a bight (bend) at the end to prevent it coming undone. Because it is easy to tie and untie, it is commonly used as a short-term lashing and in angling as a snell (a piece of hair or gut that attaches a hook to a line).

The best-known variant of this knot is the Hangman's Noose. The coils traditionally wrapped around the standing end of this form serve no useful purpose but have become emblematic of judicial murder. There are often 13 of them, a number chosen for its superstitious association with bad luck.

Another form of Noose is the Uni-knot, which is used to tie fishing lines to hooks, floats, spinners and other terminal tackle.

American singer-songwriter and musician Woody Guthrie sang about the darker uses for this kind of knot in his song 'Slipknot'.

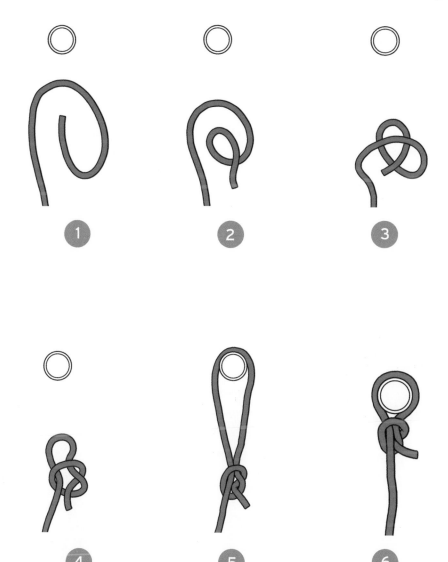

77

Overhand Knot

This one goes under numerous regional aliases: depending on where in the English-speaking world you happen to be, it may also be known as a Half Knot, an Over-and-under, a Simple Twist, a Single Knot or a Thumb Knot.

By any name it's equally easy to tie – *The Ashley Book of Knots* describes it as the simplest of its type – and its main use is as a stopper knot – one that prevents the end of a rope unravelling.

The tying method closely resembles that used in the Half Hitch (see page 52) and the first part of the Reef Knot (see page 82).

Two Overhand Knots together – known as the Double Overhand – are more effective than one alone, but no form of this knot is as strong and durable as the Ashley Stopper Knot (see page 14).

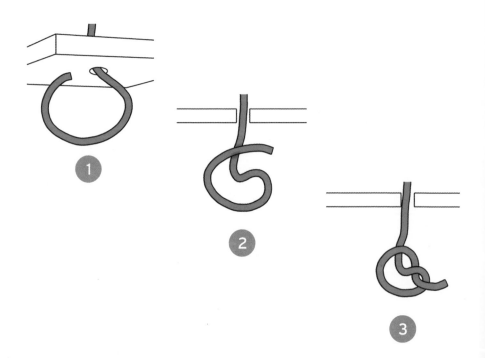

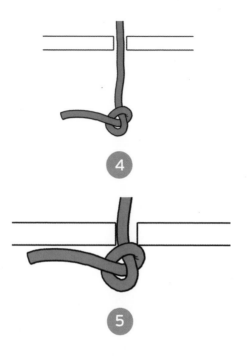

One of the simplest to form, the Overhand Knot is also one that is resistant to untying – and therefore an ideal choice where it is intended to be permanent.

Prusik Knot

This knot, sometimes inaccurately referred to as 'a Prussic' is named after Austrian mountaineer Dr Karl Prusik, who developed it in 1931.

Its main use is as a means by which a climber can progress along a guy rope by sliding another rope along it. It grips the static rope but not so tightly that it cannot be moved in either direction.

The amount of rope required to make it naturally depends on the intended purpose, but most Prusiks are on 5–6ft (1.5–1.8m) lengths.

Mountain rescuers often use the Prusik Knot to attach injured or stranded climbers to a pulley block system with a weight at the other end.

For ropes that are only ever required to slide one way along another rope, a derivative of the Prusik, the Klemheist Knot (see page 56), is generally preferred.

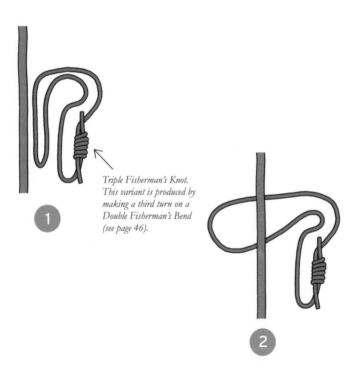

Triple Fisherman's Knot. This variant is produced by making a third turn on a Double Fisherman's Bend (see page 46).

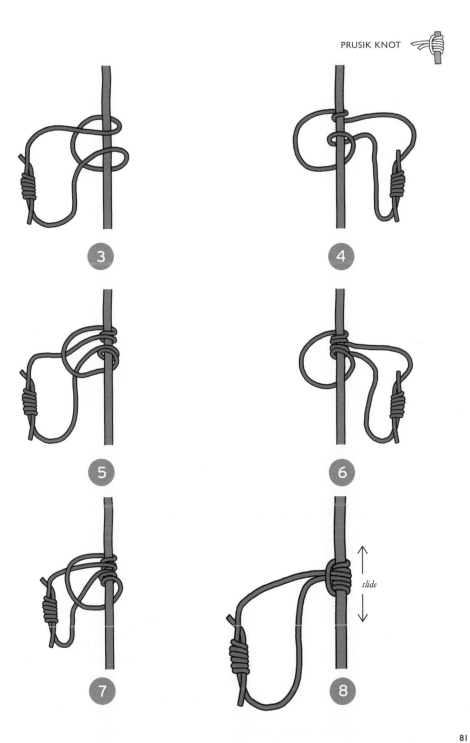

3

4

5

6

7

8

slide

Reef Knot

Although shoelaces normally end in bows, anyone who's ever tied an item of lace-up footwear has made a form of Reef Knot:

'Right over left then left over right
        Makes a knot both tidy and tight.'

(The advice is better than the scansion.)

If you do it wrong (right over left or left over right both times) you create a Granny Knot, which is inferior to the real Reef and generally regarded with pity or contempt.

The name itself comes from mariners' practice of reefing – tying down part of a sail to reduce its surface area in the face of strong winds. At the end of the storm, the Reef Knot can be undone by a pull with just one hand. It is also known as a Square Knot.

Having created the basic Reef Knot, you can develop it into more advanced and intricate bindings, such as the Surgeon's Knot shown on page 98.

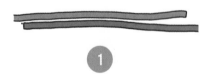

1

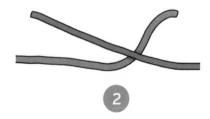

2

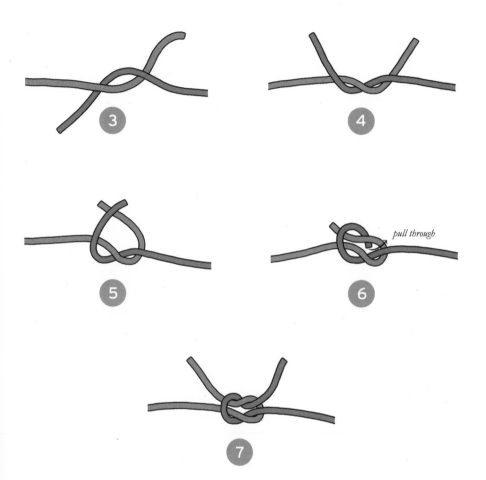

pull through

Rolling Hitch

This knot was formerly known as the Magnus Hitch or the Magner's Hitch (the etymology of both terms is obscure), and is today alternatively known as an Adjustable Hitch or a Taut-line Hitch.

Its main purpose is to enable the strain to be taken off a hawser (a rope that ties a sailing vessel to a quay) or a rope that has made a foul turn around a winch or block. It is also good for tying adjustable clothes lines.

The Rolling Hitch's great merits are that it does not bind or slip and it is one of the few knots that can be tied with a load already on it.

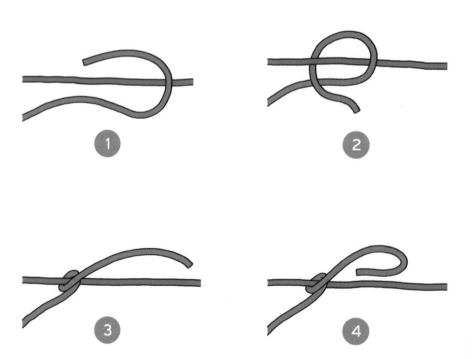

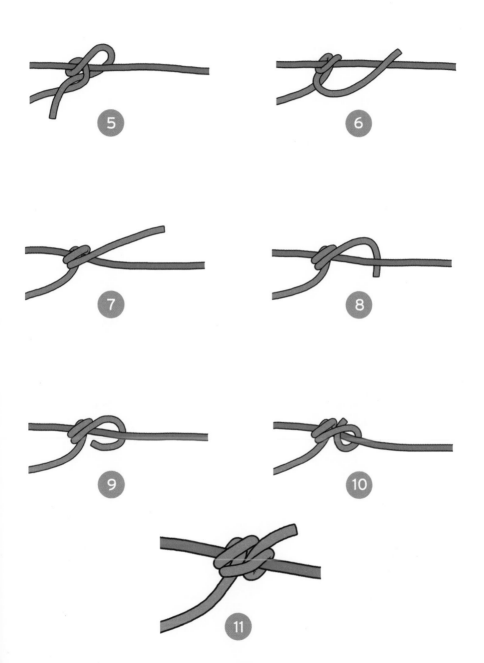

Rope Ladder Knot

Ladders with rope sides and wooden or metal rungs, such as those incorporating Marlinspike Hitches (see page 66), are fine and useful things that are not to be deprecated. However, as celebrations of the knotmaker's art they are nothing in comparison to ladders made entirely from hemp.

As the diagrams show, the rungs should be thicker than the sides; this is achieved by wrapping several loops of rope around the basic link between the uprights.

Ladders of this type are so much more adaptable than rigid alternatives; they take up very little space when not in use, and they don't smash windows or cause head injuries when the person carrying them turns round without looking.

Anyone who can make this kind of ladder can claim with justification to be a master of knotting.

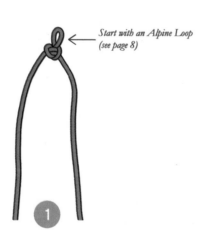

Start with an Alpine Loop (see page 8)

1

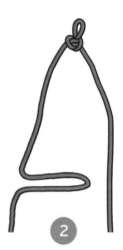

2

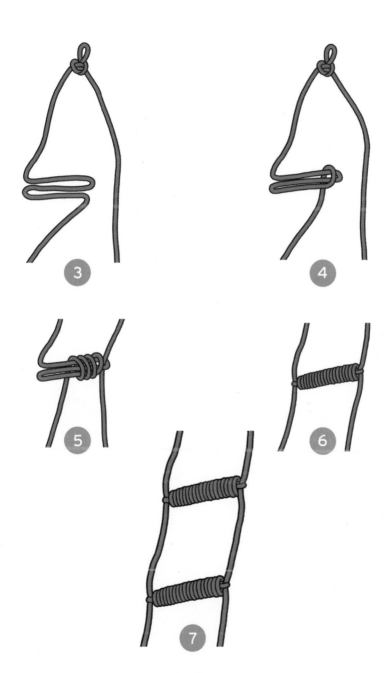

Sheepshank

This knot – named for its supposed resemblance to the leg of the animal – has virtually no use other than as a method of temporarily shortening a length of rope. It slips easily and although it might take a certain amount of weight, it cannot be relied upon to do so.

It is included here only because it is one of the six standard knots taught to Boy Scouts – the other five are the Reef Knot (page 82), the Bowline (page 21), the Sheet Bend (page 90), the Clove Hitch (page 40) and the Midshipman's Hitch (page 68). The closest functional equivalent of the Sheepshank – and one of the knots that everyone should know – is the Alpine Butterfly Loop (see page 8).

An impractical knot under load – and prone to failure if used on slippery modern synthetic rope – but one that Scouts were obliged to learn; it is sometimes applied to protect a damaged or weakened length of rope.

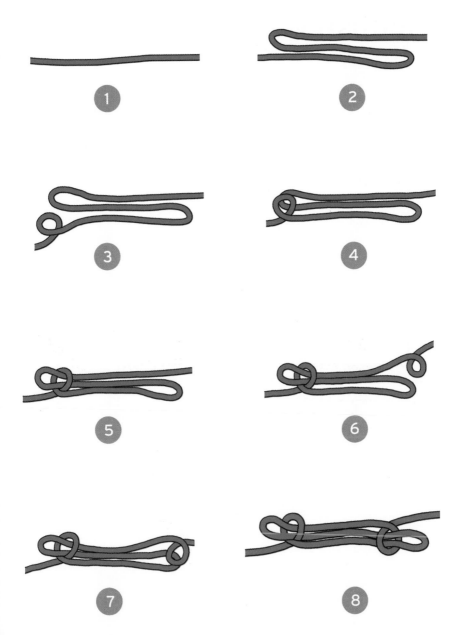

89

Sheet Bend

The Sheet Bend is used for joining two ropes of equal or unequal thickness. It is similar to the Reef Knot (see page 82), but it cannot be tied when bearing a weight.

The correct way to tie a Sheet Bend is so that both tails lie on the same side of the knot: this is the only truly dependable form; if the tails face in different directions, the knot may slip or fail.

The Sheet Bend is also known as the Becket Bend, the Common Bend, the Flag Bend, the Ordinary Bend, the Simple Hitch or the Swab Hitch.

A variant form of this knot, used on two ropes of widely different thicknesses, involves a second loop around: this is known as the Double Sheet Bend.

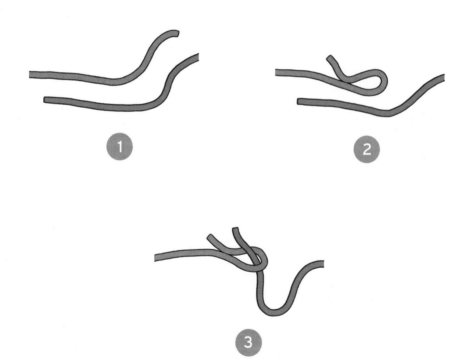

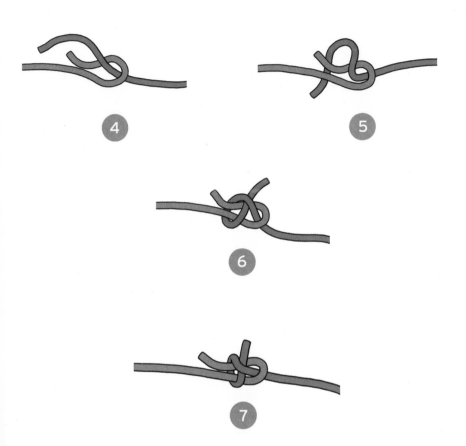

4

5

6

7

This is the classic knot
for making rope nets,
an enormously time-
consuming but ultimately
satisfying undertaking.

Square Lashing

This is an unsurpassable way of securing two poles at a fixed angle to each other.
If tied properly, square lashings are so strong that they can be used to create load-
bearing scaffolding. They are commonly used by tentless campers in the construction
of wooden-framed canvas shelters. They can also secure the horizontal bars of fences
to their stanchions. Square lashings were used extensively to bind the balsa logs of
Kon-Tiki, the raft used by Norwegian explorer Thor Heyerdahl in his 1947 expedition
across the Pacific Ocean from South America to the islands of Polynesia.

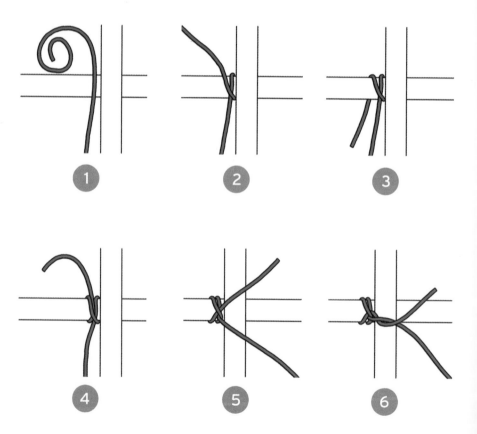

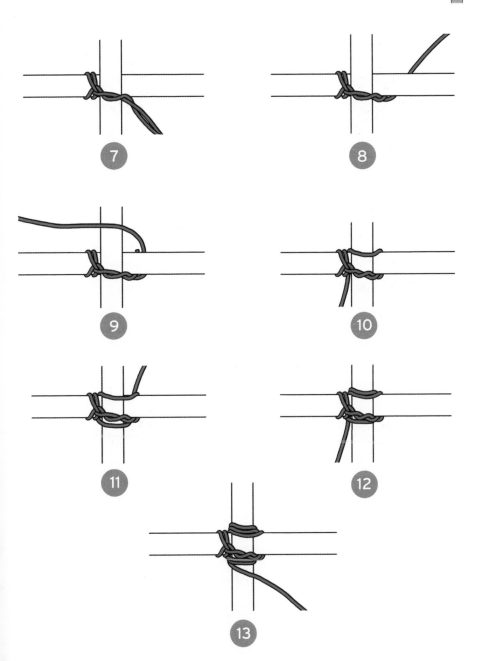

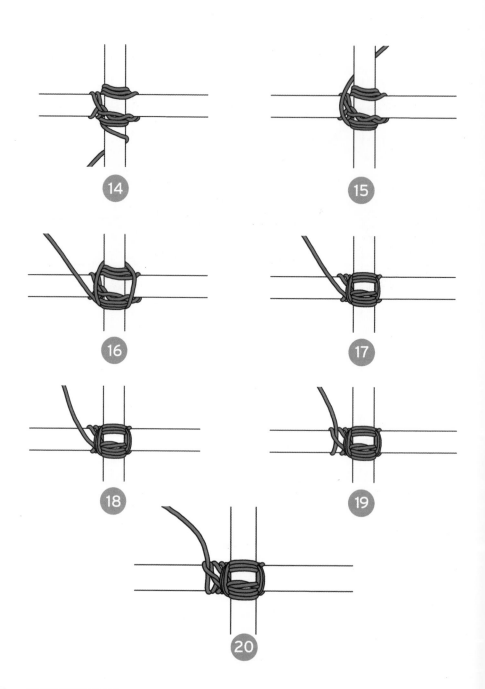

Square lashings were used to bind together the balsa logs of Thor Heyerdahl's raft, Kon-Tiki, in his epic adventure across the Pacific Ocean from South America to the Polynesian islands, in 1947.

Strangle Knot

The Strangle Knot is broadly the same as the Constrictor Knot (see page 42) and is used mainly for the same purposes: as a temporary whipping and as a drawstring for tying the mouths of sacks and bags.

However, it is not as reliable as the Constrictor and cannot be tied merely by twisting a loop. A further disadvantage is that, if it is tied slightly wrongly, it forms only a half knot after the two turns.

In addition to slipping, the other sure sign of an unsatisfactory knot is one that may easily be tightened to such a degree that it cannot be untied and can be released only by cutting; the Strangle Knot is a classic example.

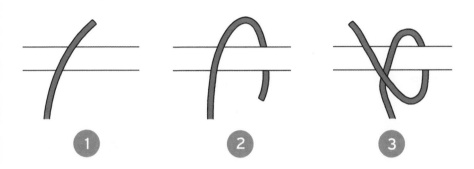

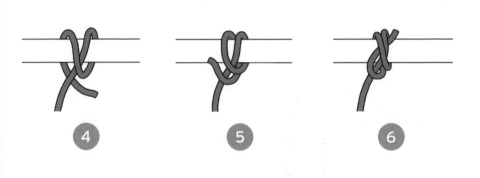

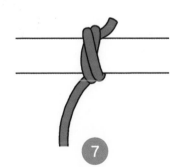

Surgeon's Knot

Also known as the Surgeon's Join, this relatively easy knot is used typically to join two ropes of uneven diameter.

The essence of the Surgeon's Knot is the two turns: it is sometimes known as a Double Surgeon's Knot, but this, as any ropemaster will tell you, is a tautology. The two component ropes can be passed through each other one more time to form a Triple Surgeon's Knot.

The key to successful tying is to ensure that all four ends are drawn together by equal simultaneous pressure.

The main shortcoming of the Surgeon's Knot is that the finished line contains a slight kink. It is therefore bulkier than the generally preferable Blood Knot (see page 18).

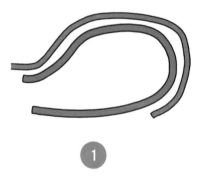

1

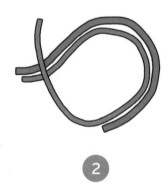

2

3

4

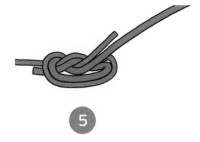

5

6

*Trim the ends of the rope
close to the knot.*

7

8

Thief Knot

Sailors traditionally used this knot to tie the ditty-bags in which they kept their personal belongings. The practice was based on the assumption that anyone who rifled through their possessions would do so in a hurry and, in haste to escape the scene of the crime, replace the Thief Knot with the superficially similar but significantly different Reef Knot (see page 82) or perhaps a Granny Knot. The only difference between a Reef Knot and a Thief Knot is that the latter's free ends are on opposite sides. The Thief Knot is known alternatively as the Draw Hitch.

In a memorable scene in the film *Dr No*, James Bond plucks a hair from his head and tapes it across the doors of the closet in his hotel so that he'll be able to tell if anyone searches his room while he's out. The Thief Knot is a maritime equivalent.

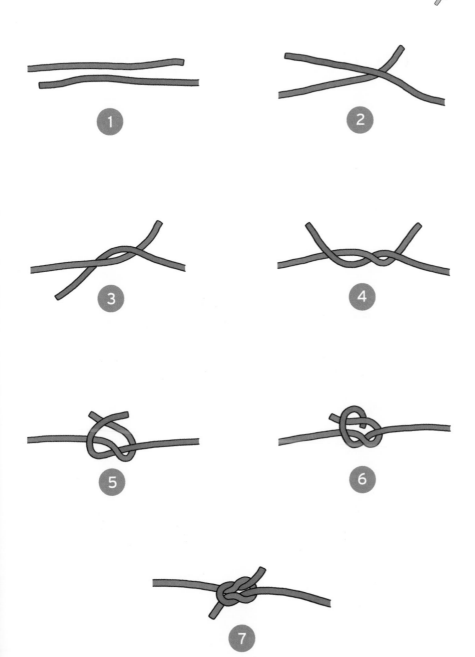

Threaded Figure Eight

This knot is strong and good-looking and an effective method either of tying two ropes together or of securing the end of a single length of rope to prevent fraying.

It is commonly tied in series at even distances along the length of ropes secured to the davits (hoists) by which ships' lifeboats are lowered into the water.

The Threaded Figure Eight takes a relatively long time to tie, but can still be quicker than a Bowline (see page 21) to link a climber to his or her carabiners (metal loops with spring-loaded gates). The standing end of a rope with a Threaded Figure Eight should be secured with a stopper knot such as an Ashley Stopper Knot (see page 14) or an Overhand Knot (see page 78).

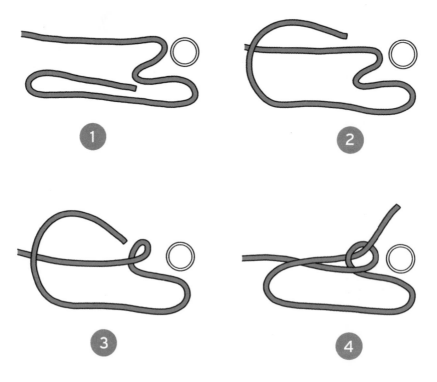

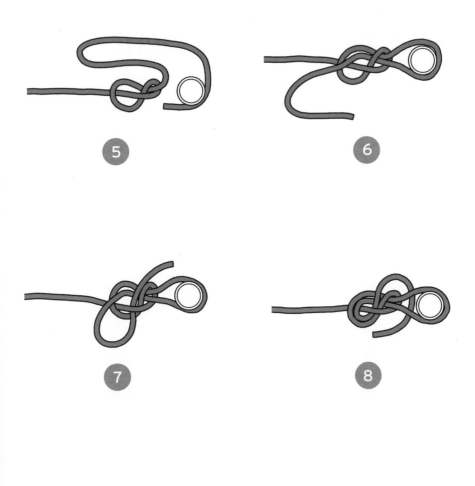

Timber Hitch

Also known as the Bowyer's Knot, the Countryman's Knot or the Lumberman's Knot, the Timber Hitch holds firmly while under stress but releases easily once the pressure is removed.

This knot is perfectly good for lifting and will not slip for as long as a steady pull is maintained. It is most widely used for towing, both at sea and on land, and by archers to attach their strings to traditional longbows made of yew. It is also the knot commonly used to tie the strings of guitars.

The earliest mention of the Timber Hitch in printed documents occurs in *A Treatise on Rigging* (circa 1625), a copy of which is preserved in the archives of Petworth House, a National Trust mansion in West Sussex, England.

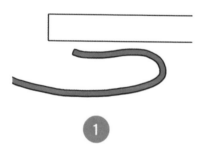

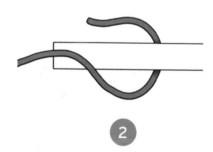

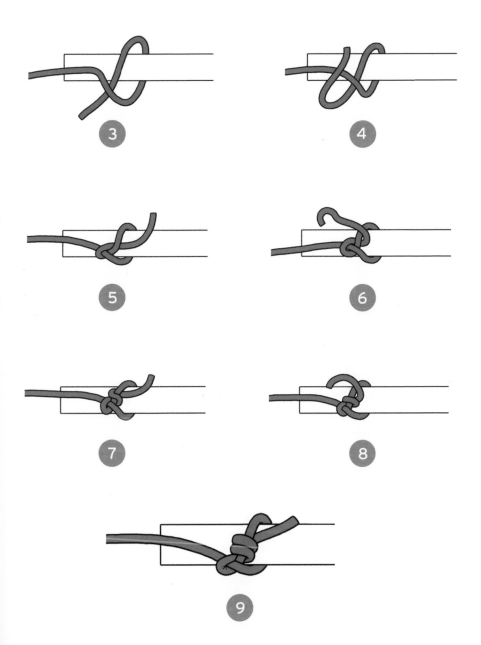

Trucker's Hitch

This knot does more than just tie: when tightened, it provides a slight mechanical advantage (an amplification of force, such as that provided by a simple lever).

There is more than one way of tying it – 'Trucker's Hitch' is thus a generic term – but it is typically as shown in the diagrams, with an eye at the top, three links to provide purchase and a hitch at the end to secure it.

The first stage is the most variable: it can be a Bowline (see page 21), an Alpine Butterfly Knot (see page 8) or not even a knot at all, but merely a twist in the rope.

The wide range of uses of this knot is reflected in its numerous bynames, which include the Harvester's Hitch, the Haymaker's Hitch, the Lorry Knot, the Power Cinch and the Wagoner's Hitch.

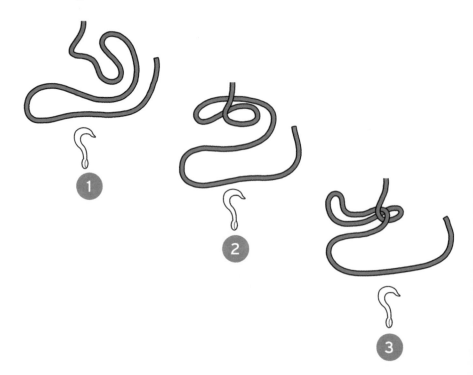

4

5

6

7

8

9

10

11

Turle Knot

William Greer Turle never claimed to have invented this knot, but it was attributed to him by H. Cholmondeley-Pennell (1837–1915) in *Modern Improvements in Fishing Tackle and Fish Hooks* (1886) and, as any modern tabloid journalist will attest, most people believe anything that is set down before them in black and white.

As can be seen from the diagrams, the Turle Knot is essentially a Double Overhand with a trimmed tag end, where the end is cut off close to the knot.

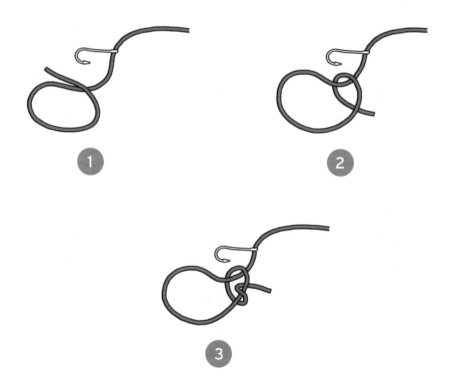

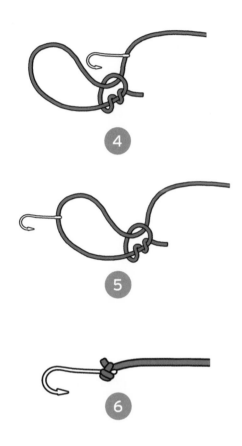

Commonly and erroneously known
as the Turtle Knot, this is named for
William Greer Turle, a 19th-century
British army officer and fisherman who
used it to tie hooks to flies and leaders.

Zeppelin Bend

The Zeppelin Bend is similar to the Ashley Stopper Knot (see page 14) – both are interlocking Overhand Knots with the ends threaded back through themselves. What gives the Zeppelin Bend the edge is that it does not jam under pressure, and is thus a useful alternative to the Double Fisherman's Bend (see page 46). The only comparably effective knots are the Alpine Butterfly Knot (see page 8) and the Carrick Bend (see page 28).

   The Zeppelin Bend must be tied just right: if it is not produced exactly as shown in the diagrams the result will be a Hunter's Bend, which is good for tying broken shoelaces but not ideal for more strenuous purposes.

The true etymology of this name is obscure, but the one most commonly put forward – that it was used to moor the early 20th-century airships – is highly improbable, not least because the knot cannot be untied under load.

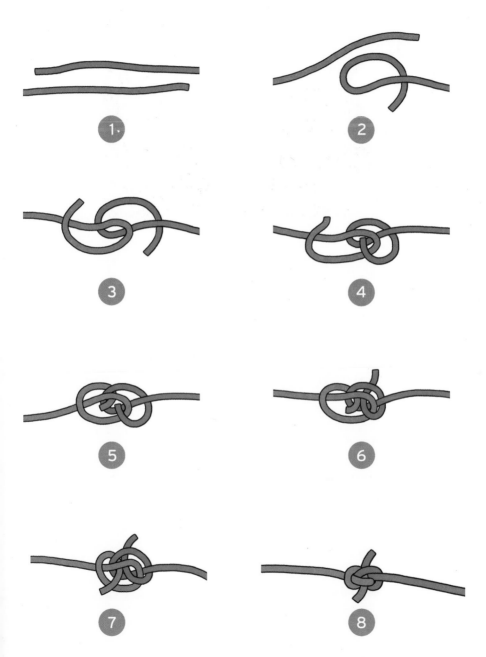

Knot tying was one of the essential skills of all traditional fishermen, such as the hardy Manxmen, who have all but disappeared. Their techniques, however, can still be passed on through the generations in tomes such as The Knot Handbook.

The author

George Lewis is the author of several books, including *Mates for Life* and *Strange Mates* (Ammonite Press) and *Castles* and *Waterfalls* (Park Lane Books). He also contributes to newspapers, magazines, encyclopedias and partworks. Lewis learned about knots in the 1950s from herring fishermen on his ancestral Isle of Man. Pupil and teachers have long gone their separate ways: the former, like most Manxmen, to the British mainland through economic necessity; the latter into the history books after the Irish Sea was trawled to near exhaustion. Lewis retains the traditional knowledge and here demonstrates that knots can give us so much more than the means to catch the traditional accompaniment to chips.

To order a book, or to request a catalogue, contact: GMC Publications Ltd
166 High Street, Lewes, East Sussex, BN7, 1XU, United Kingdom
Tel: +44 (0)1273 488005 www.gmcbooks.com